M000119413

BANG ON THE DOOR

OTHER WORKS BY THE AUTHOR
God Loves Fun
An Intimate Note to The Sincere Seeker, Vol. 1, 2, & 3
Waves of Beauty

Talks published singly:
The Language of the Heart
Prayer, the Call of the Soul
The Way Back Home
You Are the Blue Sky

The teachings of Sri Sri Ravi Shankar are available in
the form of books, video recordings and
audiotapes. For a catalog of products and to order,
contact:
Art of Living Books and Tapes
(800) 574-3001 or (515) 472-9892
Fax: (515) 472-0671
Email: aolmailorder@lisco.com

BANG
ON THE
DOOR

A collection of talks
by
Sri Sri Ravi Shankar

Published by
Art of Living Foundation
Post Office Box 50003
Santa Barbara, California 93150
Printed in the United States of America

ISBN 1-885289-31-6

Edited by Judith S. Clark

Editorial review by
Joe Puzone
Ceci Balmer

Editorial assistance by
Laura Weinberg

The master opens a door for you. Once you cross the threshold, you will find the world to be a place filled with love, joy, compassion and all virtues—and you will have no fear.

Preface

The extemporaneous talks collected in this book were given by Sri Sri Ravi Shankar during a tour of the United States. They are a call to inner transformation. They are about what is happening now. We have all heard and read the stories that happened in another time—in Buddha's time, in Jesus' time. To hear and to read is no longer enough. Now it is time to see the truth and to live it.

Here we see what is happening in the present. God is not absent, but as caring now as in the past. Grace is not less than it was. The transformation that people undergo is a living reality, a phenomenon that happens.

The poem, "Don't Move an Inch," was spoken during an East-West dialogue between Sri Sri Ravi Shankar and Fr. Thomas Keating, O.C.S.O., sponsored by The Berkeley Divinity School at Yale University. After he had offered the poem, Sri Sri turned to Father Keating and said, "You brought this forth in me."

And so, whatever your tradition, these talks are offered to bring forth the truth which lies in you, that you may give it expression in your life.

Table of Contents

Don't Move an Inch

Don't move an inch,
The journey has begun.
If you move, you are light years away.
Neither east nor west
Nor north nor south,
Don't move an inch.

Between earth and the sky—
Here—the goal dawns on you.
Don't move an inch.

Worms move through books
And birds sing His songs.
Don't move an inch.

Fill the lobbies of logic
With the smoke of Her presence.
Don't move an inch.

The roof is on
With a billion stars,
Sun and moon
Moving around you.
Don't move an inch.

Don't move an inch,
So that waves of love
May rise in your heart
And rock your life in total bliss.
I am the path, the goal and the seeker.
Don't move an inch.

DO YOU KNOW WHO YOU ARE?

I am the first and the last...
Who is like me? Let him proclaim it.

Isaiah 44:6,7

Do You Know Who You Are?

How do you introduce yourself? When someone asks, "Who are you?" do you often end up saying what you do or who you are in relation to someone else—"I'm a doctor," or "I'm so-and-so's son"?

Are you what you are doing? Is that all? You could be a tailor today. Tomorrow you could be a cook. The next day you could be a teacher. You are a parent. You have been a child. You are a student. You are a patient in bed. You have many roles to play in life, but the sum total of all the roles cannot equal you. When you identify yourself with the roles you play, you limit yourself and you are unaware of the totality, the vastness that you are.

Essentially this quest—Who am I? What is my nature?—is the beginning of the spiritual journey. The human nervous system has the capacity to inquire about itself, about the nature of living and the nature of being. This very quest is the beginning of humanness. The process of identification—I am American, I am Mexican, I am Canadian, English, German—serves some purpose, but it is not the final truth. It is not the absolute.

The spiritual journey is the search for the source. Where have I come from? What is the source of this life? All the major religions of the world move people toward this search for the source, but in the process many have gotten stuck in their positions.

Today there are wars all over the world in the name of religion. One takes a position—I am a Muslim, I am Christian, I am Hindu or Sikh or Buddhist—and then feels, Those who are not that are not mine. They don't belong to me. In the process of identifying with this position—I am a Christian or a Muslim or a Hindu—I don't even mind losing my life. That is what's happening, isn't it? Is it not sheer madness?

We call it patriotism when it comes to the question of nationality—I'm a Canadian or I'm an American. There is no difference between Canada and the United States. There is no border, nothing drawn on the earth. The land does not speak to say, "I am Canada. I am America." There is just a line on a map.

In divine creation the whole world is united. There is oneness. The search for this unity is the real spiritual journey. Unfortunately, the so-called spiritual journey has divided human beings and torn society apart.

The distinction between religion and spirituality should first become clear in our minds. I normally give the example of a banana and the banana skin: religion is like the banana skin and spirituality is the banana. People have thrown away the banana and are holding on to the skin.

Religion is outer ritual and habits, a way of life; spirituality is the quest for the source of life, going back to the source and knowing that deep within us we are part of divinity.

When this distinction becomes clear in the mind, our journey toward the source begins. It is then that we become human. It is then we become united to that principle that has enormous intelligence and orderliness and is beneath all existence, beneath every happening.

On this path everyone has to walk alone. There is no proxy walking. You cannot share someone else's walk and say, "Oh yes, I have walked there." Someone else cannot eat or drink for you. "I have drunk your tea for you, just relax." That doesn't happen. The quest is the need of the soul, of every growing soul.

Thought is a spontaneous phenomenon. It comes from some unknown corner, some unknown area of ourself. If our nervous system is stressed, then the thought that comes is distorted and we say it is negative. If the nervous system is clear, then we call the thought that comes positive, creative, life-supporting.

Intuitive thought, every scientific discovery, every work of art has sprung from that unknown area. Every poem has come out of that area. And that area is in every one of us. That is who we are. That is the true introduction to our self.

Opinions change, jobs change, relationships change, friends change. This is just a moment, a passing moment. A mood comes and goes, thoughts come and go. Whether we like it or we don't like it, things go on changing. All that there is, is change. And you identify yourself by these things that change!

Hold on to that one thing in you that does not change. Be with that. That is you. The body has changed; you have not changed. That centered point in you that does not change is the same principle that lies beneath the whole of existence, that is responsible for the orderliness of this flower, for the colors of the petals and the shape of the leaves.

When we realize this, a grand unification happens in the consciousness. Our perception changes. Anything we look at, we look at sharply. When we hear, we hear sharply. We merge with what we see and hear. There is a definite difference in the quality of perception that unites us with all that we perceive. That is why saints through all time have spoken of uniting with the ultimate, uniting with the source, uniting with the rhythm.

There are two successes: being successful in life and being successful in the world. One can be successful in the world, without necessarily being successful in life. Success in life is attending to the source and living in that joy and unconditional love.

BANG
ON
THE
DOOR

We have what we seek. It is there all the time and if we give it time, it will make itself known to us.

Thomas Merton

Bang on the Door

Two thousand years ago Jesus said, "Knock and it shall be opened unto you." At that time the human mind was simple, natural and closer to the source. One needed only to knock and the door would open. Today the mind has become more complex and more confused. Knocking will not help. One has to bang on the door.

Five thousand years ago, a person would not have needed to knock. The moment he went near the door, it would have opened, like the automatic doors at the airport that make way for you as you approach. The state of humankind five thousand years ago was much simpler than it is now.

You have never seen the door. You are stuck outside—locked out. You need to bang on your door to get into your own home. You seem to be closing your eyes, but you have never really shut your eyes. All that you are made of is from outside. Even in your sleep, the world moves in your head because you are so deeply steeped in phenomena. Complexities have kept you away from your self, from your home.

Your communication with the world is through several doors. This very body is a mansion that has many doors. Through each door you receive and you send out. The world comes into your mind through this door and goes out through that one. Through this pair of eyes, you see the whole world and you take it inside yourself. When you look at a flower, what is happening? The flower is out there, but you are capturing that inside. When you look at people, you bring all your impressions of those people inside. You are not just sitting here in front of me; you are present in my consciousness, in my mind. It becomes imprinted. All that we see we take in. Ears are also doors. The sound of a word—

mango, banana, food, donkey, madness—brings all those forms through your ears into your mind. The five senses are the five doors through which the world enters into you.

Doors are beautiful. Doors are the filters that we want and need. Sometimes we welcome in and sometimes we close out. But in one sense, our doors never close. They serve no purpose. It is like living in open space, beyond protection. In another sense, our doors have never opened. They have never opened to our innermost self. Our rationality has kept us out. When people were simple, they could directly experience things. They could feel a flower. They could look at a child and feel like a child. They could look at colors and feel joy. Our feelings have simply become words—they are not authentic, they are not coming from the source. When you look at a flower, you don't really feel its beauty. It is the mind that says, "Oh, this is beautiful." Beauty becomes a concept rather than a sensation happening within you—an explosion of wonder.

That innocent person of long ago simply had to observe creation to experience beauty. The inner chamber could open very easily. Gratefulness and gratitude could flow, and trust and faith could flower and bloom with not much effort.

Today the door to our innermost chamber is so tightly closed, we have to bang it down. Even when we trust, we trust with a doubt in it. We doubt ourselves—we do not know our own minds, we do not know how we are feeling or what is happening to us. And we have no faith that the whole universe is governed by an unseen consciousness, that an unseen power is maintaining orderliness in the clouds, the trees, the sun and moon and stars. This universe is filled with life, every inch and bit of it. We are living and we see life all around us, but we don't see the universe as a living thing. Our trust in life is not there—it simply is not there. We see only matter everywhere—objects—and we want to possess more and more. We don't see life, the living entity, everywhere. We need to bang on our door.

Five thousand years ago, people were living in a state of consciousness which enabled them to see life everywhere. It was then that they named things. Trees, even stones, were addressed as "he" or "she." (Many of the ancient languages have only two genders, masculine and feminine.) The sun, moon and stars were taken to be alive. Life was more predominant. Mind was more predominant. Consciousness was more predominant. And matter was just a wick for its expression. The glow in a candle surrounds the wick. What is most prominent, the wick or the glow?

Shut those doors through which dust comes in and open those doors through which fragments of light and love come in. When you shut one door, another door opens all by itself, and you will be filled with light, filled with love.

We know only two ways: with our doors open, we are lost in the world, lost in the dust; with our doors closed, we fall asleep. Bang on your inner door. See that there is no dearth of love in you, there is no lack of anything whatsoever inside you.

There was once a beggar who sat all his life on a particular spot. When he died, people thought that he had spoiled that piece of land. They said to each other, "Let us dig the mud from here and throw it out." When they started taking down his small hut and digging out the mud, they found an enormous hole filled with treasure. The people laughed. They said, "This man lived in poverty all his life and he was sitting on this hole filled with wealth. If he had dug down one foot right where he was, he could have been a rich man!" Everyone pitied him.

You are on the doorstep. Do not delay a moment. Bang on the door. All wealth is within you. Each one of us is the total sun. We have come into this world to contribute—to give light and love. But all of our life we remain unaware of our wealth, unaware of what we are. So don't delay. Bang on the door. Bang on the door with full force. Just knocking will not help. Get back to your self with all speed. You have been shivering outside long enough.

How are you to get back to your self—to get

home—without delay? The intensity of your wanting to get back is the first step. If you have been shivering in the cold, you won't simply sit there and knock. When you have recognized this truth—that you need to get through the door—you will have the first qualification: passion to get to the center.

When you close one door, another door opens. When you close your outside door, then your inner door opens. When you keep thinking about people, situations, circumstances, you are lost completely in that. For a moment, shut the outside door. Think only one thing: everybody is one—one person, one life. Then your outer door will close. Don't think of people in terms of personalities. Don't think this person is good, this person is bad; that person said this, the other one said that. Then you are lost. Your opinions are temporary and they cause you to worry your head.

So we shut the door towards these things, and our inner door opens and one day there is just love. That's all. Innocence, goodness and love.

GRACE
AND
GRATITUDE

In everything give thanks.

1 Thessalonians 5:18

Grace and Gratitude

A drop of water on a hot plate takes little time to disappear. It makes some noise and it evaporates. Gratitude in our life disappears even faster. We seem to forget how much we have grown and how much we have received. The mind seeks more and more. And in wanting more, it forgets the past very easily.

So gratitude rises in everyone, but disappears quickly. We cannot say that no one is grateful. Everyone is grateful, but for a moment and then it is finished.

Grace is that gratitude which remains all the time. If gratitude stays around the year like the evergreen, you can call it grace. It is like the snow in the Himalayas—whatever falls on the highest peak, stays.

When there is gratitude, complaints disappear. When complaints arise, gratitude disappears. When there is a complaint in the mind, there is discontent, frustration and depression—all that follows. If you are not grateful, you will start complaining. You will find fault. Even if there is none, you will try to see it. Your mind will find it for you. "So-and-so did not smile at me." Or, "He smiled, but it was less than a full smile."

This is the lower journey. Gratitude is the middle way. And as you rise above that, there is grace. When the gratitude in you stays, that very gratitude flows out from you as grace. Wherever you see divine grace flowing, there you will find gratitude.

I DON'T KNOW WHAT I AM SPEAKING

Tis a gift to be simple,
'Tis a gift to be free,
'Tis a gift to come down where we
     ought to be,
And when we find ourselves in the place
     just right,
'Twill be in the valley of love and delight.

                              Shaker song

I Don't Know What I Am Speaking

What is the difference between a question and wonder? For a question we seek an answer; in wonder we don't seek an answer. A question is related to sorrow; wonder is related to joy.

No one ever asks, "Why am I happy?" But when we become miserable we ask, "Why has this misery come to me?" No one ever questions why there is so much beauty in the world, but when there is dishonesty and injustice, we ask, "Why this dishonesty? Why this injustice?" This *why* comes from that area of our mind that seeks to know, that seeks knowledgeability. Knowledge-ability is labeling things.

We are born in ignorance. When we mature and we go through the process of acquiring knowledge, we again become ignorant. But there is this difference: this second *I don't know* becomes a beautiful *I don't know*. It is wonder. Why this creation? I don't know. What is happening? I don't know.

What you know, you speak from your intellect, from your knowledge. But the purpose of knowledge is to make you aware of how ignorant you are. The more you know, the more unknown remains. So, in fact, the unknown grows—what we don't know grows.

I don't know what I am speaking. An ignorant person talks and he doesn't know what he says. So, also, an enlightened person talks and he doesn't know what he says. If he knows and talks, the words are coming from limitation. If he doesn't know and talks, he allows the words to flow through. He is open. He remains available to that area of the self, the consciousness, from which the words come. Any enlightened person can speak on any subject that he doesn't know. If you asked Kabir or St. Francis to write a thesis, they would be unable to do it, but they could sit and let poetry flow through.

What you have known and then speak is stale, but when you speak what you don't know, it is something fresh and new. Talking about what you know may be creative, but definitely less creative than when you talk about something that you don't know. In that moment, you allow yourself to be a doorway for the creative process to spring through you. We are all just doors. Every parent is a door for a new soul to enter into the world—nothing more than a door. Every artist is a door for some work of art to flow through them. All your virtues, all beauty, all that is truth spring from the same source—one source. That is why I say, "I don't know what I speak." Knowing, knowledgeability, limits.

The highest knowledge is called "the end of knowledge." *Vedanta* means "truth, the end of knowledge." It is the same with truth as with appreciation of beauty and the expression of love: they cannot be practiced. Truth can only be cognized, recognized, felt, experienced and lived, moment to moment.

Observing the unpredictability of life, the unpredictability of the world, creates an awe in you, a sense of wonder. Every person on this earth feels completely helpless at some time or other, whether he is John F. Kennedy, Mahatma Ghandi, or someone on the street. Everyone feels that things are ruled by something other than what can be logically conceived. When we feel helpless, we tend to become frustrated and cynical. At this juncture the feeling of helplessness can turn into prayer or can turn into deeper frustration. Divinity can be perceived in the prayerfulness. In frustration, we become more and more disheartened.

Prayer is not a practice; it is a happening. When from the very core of your heart you feel helplessness, that is prayer. When you are successful and you know it, a sense of doership comes. I don't mean that we should all be miserable in order to pray, but when the feeling of helplessness does arise, prayer can be very authentic. This authentic prayer can bring up a power within us that can transform life.

When we recognize our helplessness, we need to put a distance between ourself and what is happening. I am talking and yet I am watching myself talk. I am sitting here, yet I am not just sitting here. I have entered all the things here—the cushions, the carpet, the walls, the photograph. All over it is me, an expanded awareness living life from that area beyond calculation.

We measure and talk. We calculate, we prepare and we talk. But when we talk of something which we don't know, it is very adventurous. I have never read the Bible, but I can speak on the Bible. Nor have I ever read Buddha, but I can speak about Buddha. Being that state of consciousness allows knowledge to flow through. And this ability is within every one of us.

You have heard and read that ego is bad, that ego is an obstruction to spiritual growth, an obstruction to knowledge. Ego is nothing but being unnatural. Naturalness is being at home and feeling close to everyone. Ego is distance—ego means that I don't consider you as a part of me so I keep a distance. When I have to show off to you or behave a certain way, there is no cordiality, no love, no connection. Then the ego comes into play.

Being like a child, feeling at home, making everybody one's own, dropping defenses and boundaries—that is being natural. You feel light and wonderful within yourself. People may think you are a little crazy—it doesn't matter. Your mind is saved. At any cost you need to save your mind. Just meditating and doing some practices will not help you unless you also guard the mind from the dust which flies in from the world.

Maintaining naturalness, innocence, in spite of intelligence is enlightenment. It has great value. If a person who has a lot of responsibility says, "I do nothing," that has great value. When someone who is very lazy says, "I do nothing," it has no value. If someone who is doing all the time and has great responsibility can say, "I do nothing," then that person's consciousness has taken a shift. An ignorant person being innocent has no value. When intelligence and innocence go together, a beauty dawns.

As our intelligence grows, we tend to become crooked. What our world needs is not more intelligence. There is enough intelligence. What the world is missing is innocence. The value of innocence is being destroyed. And that innocence is egolessness, naturalness.

What is happening in your mind right now? Are you aware of yourself listening to me? No. There are two possibilities here. Either you are simply listening to whatever I am saying, or there is a debate going on—yes, no, yes, no. You agree with me on what you already know. You say, "Yes, yes, I agree." And to what you don't know, you say, "No, how could it be?" In this case you are actually listening to your own self. With this tape playing in your head, you only know what you already know. And you are not really listening to me at all! Whether you agree or disagree with whatever I say doesn't matter. But are you aware of what is happening in your own mind? That is what is important. Awareness of this process happening within you is self-study.

If you observe further, you will see that every emotion, every thought creates a sensation in a particular place in your body. It takes a little practice, but soon the mind becomes hollow and empty. Through that empty space, truth dawns. That is why *I don't know* is beautiful. The moment you think, "I know," then the mind is not yet hollow and empty. Knowledge, the labeling of things, has come into play.

Blessed are those who are confused. Confusion means your previous knowledge has broken down, your belief has broken down. Space is created. The mind goes blank. That is a step toward true knowledge.

In India, you don't find signboards everywhere. If you ask for directions, people will tell you which way to go whether they know or not. They may be completely wrong, but they don't feel comfortable saying, "I don't know." So they may send people in just the opposite direction from where they wanted to go.

The beautiful *I don't know*. Innocence. That is what is needed today.

ALWAYS CONNECTED TO GOD

The color of a wall depends on the wall. In the same manner the existence of creatures depends on the love of God. Separate the color from the wall and the color would cease to be. So all creation would cease to exist if separated from the love that God is.

Meister Eckhart

Always Connected to God

Whenever one has to talk about God, the limitation of words and language becomes very evident. Truth cannot be captured by words. The words you use to indicate a connection to God also indicate a separation from God. If you say you are connected, it indicates that in some way you have been outside of God—that you have existed as something separate and are being connected. This is not so.

You are like the fish in the ocean. The moment the fish comes out of the water, life comes out of the fish—a corpse of a fish comes out of the water, not the fish itself. The fish cannot exist outside the ocean, just as waves cannot exist apart from the ocean. As the life of a fish is inseparable from the ocean, you are inseparable from God.

The two words *always* and *connected* do not go together. If you say "always" and then "connected," the word *connected* loses its meaning. The existence of God is beyond time. To indicate that, you can use the word *always*: God is always. But when you say you are always connected to God, you make yourself separate from God. That is why I say language is inadequate.

Whenever Buddha was asked to speak about God, he kept silent. It was not that he didn't know. Many people thought that Buddha was an atheist because he never spoke of God. He was not an atheist. It is simply that he knew the profundity of truth and the inadequacy of words.

If you subtract one portion of a circle, the circle is not complete. If you subtract one thing from God, God no longer remains. But the nature of your mind is to dissect and divide. The moment you divide, duality happens. A word appears. Two appear. And the two become many. In many, you are lost.

In Sanskrit *fear* means "two." How does fear come? Because of some division, because of recognition of separateness. Division means taking one thing in and separating something out. Accepting and rejecting. Your rejecting, your separating causes fear, and fear is unbearable to life. Separation does not exist. You cannot separate. It is an illusion in the mind. In recognizing the oneness, fear vanishes.

You have two options: either you feel you are connected to God, to the master, to existence; or you feel you *are* God, you *are* the master, you *are* existence. Then laughter, dance and joy dawn in life.

For a long, long time you have taken the first option and felt that you are separate from the whole of existence. This is a hypnotism that you have undergone. You have to de-hypnotize yourself and know that you are part of the truth, you are part of this whole.

Have you ever sat on a rock and thought of yourself as a part of this earth? This body has come out of the substance of this earth. What is this body? Proteins, amino acids, carbohydrates, minerals, salt. It is all part of this earth. And this body is going to go back into this earth one day.

And this earth is as lively as you think you are. You know you are alive because you act and you react to situations and people. But the trees are also alive. They, too, react. Recently botanists have discovered that trees express fear and are sensitive, although the degree of their expression of that is less than yours. This earth holds millions of different species of life and billions of bacteria. This very soil is alive. Life is present in every pore of this earth. That is how it can bring life into manifestation in a body.

You have life in every cell of your body—the skin, the hair, the whole body. You may be unaware of yourself as you sit in front of the television, completely lost in phenomena or lost in your mind. But with your awareness on it or not, life is present in every cell of your body in this moment.

Be aware that your body is part of this earth. Ninety percent of your body is water. The water in you has the same percentage of saline, the same contents, as the water in the ocean. You are encapsulated ocean living outside the ocean. And the breath which is going in and out of your body is part of the air covering the earth. There is no new air. One ancient air is being recirculated.

You are part of existence. Your mind is just a fragment of expression of the whole big mind and creation. When this awareness comes, then the small *I* with which you are thinking "I, I, I, I, me, me," transforms into a big *I* or no *I*.

I wouldn't say you are always connected to the earth; I would say you are part of this earth. Have you ever thought, as you sat at your dining table and took a loaf of bread in your hand,

"This is my body. This bread that is going inside me will become the cells in my body. This bread is my future body—it is just a matter of time"? You have a cup of milk in front of you. Have you ever thought, "This, too, is part of my body. This milk is going to be my blood"? When Jesus started the mass, he said, "This is my flesh. This is my blood." He meant, "This entire creation is my body."

Feel one with everything. You are already part of the food you eat. Even before eating it, you are part of it. It is already your flesh. Jesus told his followers, "Don't lament. Don't think I am just in this body. This bread is my body. And all the food in the world is my body, because this food becomes my body."

What is the big thing about the body? When this body goes, another body will come because the food is there always. The food creates the body.

If you eat food with all awareness, I am you. This consciousness, this awareness that is me that you feel is so beautiful, is in you too. You don't lack a thing that I have.

This body is not my flesh. This bread is my flesh. This flesh is this bread. Know the difference between the physical body and the flesh, and this entire world becomes your body. That is cosmic consciousness.

All are mine—as much mine as my own finger. Everyone is part of me.

When you know everyone is a part of you, then all your cravings disappear, all your aversions disappear. Your cravings come because you think you don't have. Your aversions come because you don't want to have what you think you have. Do you see the irony of it? When you know everything already belongs to you, your cravings subside. When you know whatever you are averse to is part of you, then aversion disappears and total synthesis happens. Unity dawns.*

---

*This understanding of cravings and aversions applied to the situations of daily life becomes a valuable spiritual practice.

Even the word *unity* is not the right word. That also indicates a duality. If you can say one, there has to be two. So I say language is inadequate to express any truth about existence. It is better to keep silent.

TRUE INTIMACY

Human nature was originally one and we were a whole. And the desire and pursuit of the whole is called love.

Plato

True Intimacy

True intimacy is one-sided and nonjudgmental. It starts from inside.

In true intimacy, you do not look at whether the other person loves you or not, whether the other person treats you well or not. I say that is none of my business. If I want to be intimate with someone, I take it for granted that they feel they love me. When you doubt whether the other person loves you, then your love for that person goes down.

There is no way you can know the love of another person. If you look only at the expression of love, you will be mislead. Someone may say,

"Oh, you are so wonderful, I love you so much." And if you think they mean that, you may be mistaken. Or if you think someone who doesn't say, "Oh, I love you so much," really doesn't love you, then, too, you may be mistaken. Action does not always represent the truth of the state of being.

In true intimacy you stop looking at the act and you start being in love. If you have determined to love someone, do not even think about whether they love you or not. You love them. That is enough. They may behave badly toward you. They may test you to see whether the love in you is true or not. Even then you give back love.

Take it for granted that everyone in creation and everything in creation loves you, because everything has come out of love and goes back to love and remains in love. Then you are flowing with the current of the river. If you don't see that, then you are going against the current and you will not be loving.

You are already intimate. You cannot be any
more intimate. Your wanting to be intimate, or
to have more intimacy, is a block. In looking out
there for intimacy, you are swimming against
the current. That brings you strain, frustration,
anger. True intimacy is coming back to the self.

In creation everything experiences intimacy—
everything other than human beings, that is.

When the human mind is stressed and tense, it
judges, discriminates, loves this, doesn't love
that, makes one hundred boundaries, *if's* and
but's, doubts, and removes itself from existence.
This apparent removal of existence from the
flow of existence is called separation. Oneness
with existence is intimacy.

All modes and moods are included in true intimacy. Love is not always goody-goody and saying nice things. It is saying unpleasant things,
too. Getting angry at times, even fighting, is also
love. This morning I got a phone call from
India. They said, "Come back quickly. It is too
cold for you there. When you return, we will

lock you up and not let you go." They were literally fighting with me on the phone. That is also out of love. Demand, with awareness, also comes out of love.

You are trying to swim against the current, but the current is so strong that you move with it. Intimacy is recognizing the direction of the current and being with the direction, feeling that you are totally loved. Everything in you is rising out of love and love only.

You demand love, but how much have you been giving? If you feel you have been contributing enough, loving enough, then you are not loving enough. In love you always feel inadequacy: "I have not loved enough. I have not done enough." When this gets turned around, then you say, "I have loved enough. What did I get in return? I have not been cared for." These demands will start. When you switch your direction, the struggle begins. True intimacy is recognizing the flow of the current and joyfully floating with it. The current is there. You don't have to swim. It is effortless.

In true intimacy there is dispassion. Observe your mind. What is happening in there? Likes and dislikes, wanting and not wanting—I want this, I don't want this—constant debate, cynicism, criticism, apathy, dejection. Are you aware of all these fluctuations happening in the mind? For awhile, throw off everything. Just sit. That is dispassion, being centered.

After laughing a lot and being very excited, have you observed that the excitement cannot be held in your mind? It begins to be too much. You want to throw off the excitement and just be quiet for awhile. What big joy can you ever keep? Wisdom dawns the day you recognize that joy is painful. Your dispassion begins on that day when you notice joy is disturbing.

We have lost that sensitivity. That is why there is so much craving for joy, for something bigger: "There must be something better for me, something to give me more happiness." This is feverishness. So you move from this feverishness to that feverishness and from that to this. It is a constant struggle.

Sorrow brings feverishness and joy brings feverishness. Dispassion is that delicate balance that is beyond both joy and sorrow. In dispassion any great joy can come up and it will not shake you. Even if you are offered the heavens, you won't move an inch from your seat. That is enlightenment. Dispassion is the secret.

You can learn to meditate and you can learn other techniques, but dispassion you cannot learn. It can only blossom in your life, in time or through the presence of your master. There is no other way dispassion can blossom. You cannot get it in books. Only experience will teach you.

The highest wisdom that can be achieved on this planet is dispassion. Anything can be shaken, but not dispassion. Anything can be bought, but not dispassion. The only rich one is the one who has dispassion.

Suppose someone approaches you and says, "If you tell this lie, I'll give you two million dollars." Just imagine what you would do! Your mind will put forward one hundred and one justifications. You'll say, "Okay, so what. If I say this, some good may come from it—I'll use the two million dollars for the benefit of humankind. I don't want it for myself, but I can do some good work for the whole world." You will be tempted. You will move from your position. But one who is dispassionate cannot be moved.

Once a prostitute was asked to tell some lies about Kabir, the famous Indian saint. She was a very conscientious woman and she didn't want to speak a lie. The people said to her, "It is nothing. When Kabir gives satsang, you just go to him and hug him. Say, 'Oh, my dear, I have not been with you in so many days.' Just say that." The people tempted her to do this for two gold coins. When she did it, Kabir said, "Oh, I have been waiting for you. Where have you been?" When Kabir spoke in this way to the prostitute, she was shocked.

Kabir was not a literate man—he was a weaver, an innocent man—but the Brahmanjñana knowledge was dawning on earth through him.

He gave satsangs every night—so beautiful, so wonderful. This event threw many people off balance, but Kabir welcomed it: "I have been missing you, too. Come and sit." People left Kabir after this incident because their intimacy was just with the words. It was not true intimacy—it was not one-sided. One event was sufficient to turn them around.

The King of Benares called for an inquiry. "What is happening? Is this man a fake or is he a real saint?" After a week this woman could not remain silent. She went to the King and confessed what she had done. Her whole life was then transformed.

Dispassion always reveals the truth. If you want to know the truth of something, be very dispassionate, centered—so centered. That is strength. True intimacy can happen only in dispassion.

Dispassion is not a flat uninteresting state of mind or a negative mood. Dispassion is not a dull state. Many people think that dispassion means being very stiff and removed. No. Only dispassion is intimate.

In dispassion you are intimate with yourself. Then you can be intimate with everyone else. If you are totally integrated in yourself, you can love and you can be intimate with anyone else without any difficulty. Then criticism, cynicism and disinterestedness all disappear. Disinterest is different from dispassion. Your disinterest is because of passion.

The moment you become dispassionate, there is nothing but love. There is nothing but intimacy. There is no two.

FOOTSTEPS

Footsteps

Below you will find excerpts from other talks given by Sri Sri Ravi Shankar. They illustrate the practical wisdom that he offers to guide our feet on the path.

Spiritual practice

The point of all spiritual practice is to smile authentically from your heart, to drop your judgmental mind and be friendly. How do you relate to yourself? Can you relate in the same way to everyone else? They are all part of you. If you are able to give some peace, some love, some joy to the people around you, then you are moving in a spiritual direction.

God

Love, beauty and truth are all beyond proof. Nobody can prove them. And nobody can prove God. If someone tries to prove that God is, they are taking a disastrous step. Whatever you can prove, you can disprove also. God is beyond our proof and disproof. God is an experience.

Love

Love is not an act; it is the very state of your being. In deep meditation, we see that everyone is part of ourself. Then the flow of love happens naturally. It's not superimposed. It's not a cultivated, artificial love. It's the state of your existence.

There is an old saying that the lane of love is very narrow. Two cannot fit there. Either there is love or there is you. Love is forgetting "What about me?" and dissolving. You are looking at the vast sky—so many stars, the moon, the sun—but if a small particle of dust gets into your eye, all of that is blotted out. In that same way, the small "me, me, me, me" covers your infinite nature, the unbounded love that you are.

Gratitude

You cannot be grateful and feel lack. The two cannot occur at the same time. When you feel grateful, you feel full, "great-full," and complaint, discontent, frustration and depression all disappear. The gratefulness in you is beautiful. When it blossoms, it attracts the angels and all the devas, rishis and saints. The cosmic beings are charmed by that beauty and rejoice in it.

Peace

You want peace, but you have become restless

wanting peace. In wanting everyone to be peaceful, you have created turmoil. Peace comes from within, not from without. If you are peaceful, your environment becomes peaceful and the people around you become peaceful. You are the center of the universe.

Worry

Streams of thoughts pass through your mind—they come and they go. You may catch hold of one of those thoughts and not allow it to go. When one thought is stuck in your mind like a needle stuck in the groove of an old gramophone record, that is called worry. And worry causes sorrow. All sorrow arises from getting stuck in an event or thought or desire that is past.

Longing

Longing comes from gratefulness. It does not come out of complaint or frustration.

Complaints and frustration bring anger and hatred. Only gratefulness can bring longing.

On the spiritual path, longing may come up and it may be there for some time. This may be necessary so that you can stop looking here and there, here and there. In longing, focus will come automatically. The heart is drawn in, the mind is charmed. Longing is a gift to help you on your way.

Suffering

When you feel happy and dance and sing, that is true prayer. That is true meditation. Meditation is a fountain of joy and ecstasy. People glorify suffering. The Divine enjoys your happiness more.

Karma

Grace and knowledge can cut the bondage of karma. Otherwise there is no end to it. Good karmas will produce good karmas. Bad karmas will produce bad karmas, bad actions. Due to bad karma, you are engaged in bad actions, and these bad actions will, in turn, create bad karma—action and its results, action and its results. It can continue forever, but if you are more aware and more centered, you can burn karma.

Dispassion

All that is belongs to the Divine, so drop all that you carry. "I am insulted. This wrong thing has been done to me." You see intention behind every action. Simply drop all that. Let it be. Flow with the moment and life will smooth out on its own.

Criticism

Doubt people's compliments, but do not doubt their criticism. Criticism is harder to give than praise, so a person may be quite sincere if they make a critical comment to you. There may be false motives behind praise, yet we long for others to praise us. When you become centered and calm within the depth of yourself, praise will come to you naturally.

Money

If money is your goal, then everything in life becomes meaningless—even money itself! If love is your goal, everything becomes more meaningful. A person who is worried about money is fearful, and fear blocks out love. The opposite is also true—if there is love, there is no fear. Then you don't worry about money. You do whatever is needed in a relaxed manner. Fear has no basis. All is being taken care of in this world.

Ambition

Ambition is poisonous to joy and love in life. We have a wrong notion that only when we have ambition or desire will we be able to make progress. This is not so. You can make better progress without this feverishness. What can root out ambition? Look at it. See it is futile. You can be happy now, right now, wherever you are, and still progress in life.

Past lives

Unless your mind gets thoroughly established in the present moment, you do not remember past lives. And when your mind is so thoroughly in the present moment, any memory of the past doesn't matter. You ask me if life is infinite and eternal. These are the words you have heard or read. Don't worry about eternity. Know you are here now. Just experience this time.

Wonder

Someone who loves science or mathematics and is devoted to its study will be overwhelmed by the complexity of creation. If you love astronomy and go deeply into it, you will ask, "How many billion planets are there? How many billion stars? How many solar systems? What is time? How many years has all of this existed?" It shakes you. It stuns you. In that moment, you wonder. And the wonder brings love in you.

Enlightenment

You ask, "Can a Christian or a Westerner be enlightened?" If someone thinks he is a Christian, he is a Hindu, he is a Moslem—he is somebody—then he cannot be enlightened. As long as anyone takes such a position, then enlightenment is far away. A human being can be enlightened, not a Christian, a Hindu or a Moslem. Do you see the difference? If you know you are just a human being and if you know you are just Being, you are already enlightened.

Silence

Silence purifies speech. If you are talking all the time, you lose awareness of the effect of your words. Most of the problems around you are caused by talking. Talk less, but with more awareness. Every word you use, use purposefully.

Change

Nothing belongs to you—not your body, not your thoughts or emotions or feelings. None of these are yours. They come on their own, stay for awhile and go on their own. Remember that your nature, which is joy and peace and fulfillment, remains the same for eternity.

Go Beyond

Move beyond ignorance,
Beyond knowledge.
Move beyond doubt,
Beyond trust.
Move beyond time,
Beyond space.
Move beyond hate,
Beyond love.
That is your true realm.
That is where you came from.
That is where you exist.

Go beyond light,
Beyond darkness.
That is the realm of your true being.

For information about Art of Living courses, workshops
and programs, contact a center closest to you:

Africa
Hema & Rajaraman
Art of Living
P.O.Box 1213
Peba Close Plot 5612
Gaborone, Botswana
Tel. 26-735-2175
Aolbot@global.co.za

Canada
Fondation L'Art de Vivre
B.P. 170
13 Chemin du lac Blanc
St. Mathieu-du-Parc,
Quebec   GOX 1NO
Tel. 819-532-3328
Artofliving.northamerica@
Sympatico

Germany
Akadamie Bad Antogast
Bad Antogast 1
77728 Oppenau
Germany
Tel. 49-7804-910-923
Artofliving.Germany@
t-online.de

India
Vyakti Vikras Kendra
(Art of Living)
No. 19, 39 A Cross
11th Main Road
4th T block, Jayanagar
Bangalore 560041, India
Tel. 91-808-432-274

Singapore
N. Vijaykumar /Art of Living
#03-09 The River Walk
20 Upper Circular Road
Singapore 058416
Tel. 65-438-1900
Chaykk@singnet.com.sg

United States
Art of Living Foundation
P.O. Box 50003
Santa Barbara, CA 93150
Tel. 800-897-5913
www.artofliving.org